BROTHER

by

Lisa Ebersole

SAMUEL FRENCH, INC.

From the Reviews of
BROTHER
by
Lisa Ebersole

"As a theater experience, *BROTHER* is refreshing. The cast is proficient and easy to watch, and the play's brevity and suggestiveness make it continually engaging."
—*The New York Times*

"Bang the gongs: American theatre has found a rare new voice in Lisa Ebersole, who wrote, directed, and performs in the short, tense drama *BROTHER*. Every beat is fraught with interest and impact. Ebersole presents a world that is both recognizable and entirely her own." —*Back Stage*

"Finally, etiquette dilemmas worthy of our day and age: Just how many racist slurs should you fling at a guest before clubbing him to death? And should you sleep with him first? Daring to answer, Lisa Ebersole's *BROTHER* watches four disaffected youths experimenting with varieties of abuse."
—*Time Out, New York*

"Take two couples, a late-night party, far too much booze, sexual tension and verbal abuse, and what do you get?... a strange, unsettling new play written and directed by Lisa Ebersole called *BROTHER*." —*NY1 News*

"In the manner of Neil LaBute and Patrick Marber, Ebersole doesn't shy away from questions of racism and social injustice."
—*TheatreMania.com*

BROTHER

by

Lisa Ebersole

SAMUEL FRENCH, INC.

45 West 25th Street
NEW YORK 10010
LONDON

7623 Sunset Boulevard
HOLLYWOOD 90046
TORONTO

Copyright © 2006 by Lisa Ebersole

ALL RIGHTS RESERVED

CAUTION: Professionals and amateurs are hereby warned that BROTHER is subject to a royalty. It is fully protected under the copyright laws of the United States of America, the British Commonwealth, including Canada, and all other countries of the Copyright Union. All rights, including professional, amateur, motion picture, recitation, lecturing, public reading, radio broadcasting, television and the rights of translation into foreign languages are strictly reserved. In its present form the play is dedicated to the reading public only.

The amateur live stage performance rights to BROTHER are controlled exclusively by Samuel French, Inc., and royalty arrangements and licenses must be secured well in advance of presentation. PLEASE NOTE that amateur royalty fees are set upon application in accordance with your producing circumstances. When applying for a royalty quotation and license please give us the number of performances intended, dates of production, your seating capacity and admission fee. Royalties are payable one week before the opening performance of the play to Samuel French, Inc., at 45 W. 25th Street, New York, NY 10010; or at 7623 Sunset Blvd., Hollywood, CA 90046, or to Samuel French (Canada), Ltd., 100 Lombard Street, Lower Level, Toronto, Ontario, Canada M5C 1M3.

Royalty of the required amount must be paid whether the play is presented for charity or gain and whether or not admission is charged.

Stock royalty quoted upon application to Samuel French, Inc.

For all other rights than those stipulated above, apply to to Fifi Oscard Agency, Inc., 110 West 40th Street, New York, NY 10018.

Particular emphasis is laid on the question of amateur or professional readings, permission and terms for which must be secured in writing from Samuel French, Inc.

Copying from this book in whole or in part is strictly forbidden by law, and the right of performance is not transferable.

Whenever the play is produced the following notice must appear on all programs, printing and advertising for the play: "Produced by special arrangement with Samuel French, Inc."

Due authorship credit must be given on all programs, printing and advertising for the play.

ISBN 0 573 63224 3   Printed in U.S.A.

No one shall commit or authorize any act or omission by which the copyright of, or the right to copyright, this play may be impaired.

No one shall make any changes in this play for the purpose of production.

Publication of this play does not imply availability for performance. Both amateurs and professionals considering a production are *strongly* advised in their own interests to apply to Samuel French, Inc., for written permission before starting rehearsals, advertising, or booking a theatre.

No part of this book may be reproduced, stored in a retrieval system, or transmitted in any form, by any means, now known or yet to be invented, including mechanical, electronic, photocopying, recording, videotaping, or otherwise, without the prior written permission of the publisher.

BILLING AND CREDIT REQUIREMENTS

All producers of *BROTHER must* give credit to the Author of the Play in all programs distributed in connection with performances of the Play, and in all instances in which the title of the Play appears for the purposes of advertising, publicizing or othewise exploiting the Play and /or a production. The name of the Author *must* appear on a separate line on which no other name appears, immediately following the title and *must* appear in size of type not less than fifty percent of the size of the title type.

BROTHER was first presented at The Paradise Factory in New York City on July 21, 2005 by Tom Noonan. The cast and creative contributors were:

MARGEAUX............................Stephanie Sanditz
JAMIE..Lisa Ebersole
CARL...Orran Farmer
KEVIN...Haskell King

Director..Lisa Ebersole
Producer..Luke Rosen
Stage Manager........................Margaret Bodriguian
Assistant Director..................................Alex Simon
Producer's Assistant......................Brian Gillespie
Set Design.......................................Bret Haines
Costumes..............................Hannah Holdsworth
Lighting..Greg Balla
Fight Coordinator..........................Chris Chaberski
Production Assistant..................................TJ Craig

The production was made possible
with generous support from
Avraham Kadar, M.D.

CHARACTERS

JAMIE: A white woman in her late 20s.
CARL: A black man 20 - 35.
MARGEAUX: A white woman in her mid 20s, JAMIE's sister.
KEVIN: A white man in his late 20s, JAMIE's husband.

Note: the ages of the characters are not rigid as long as they are consistent—Jamie and Margeaux should look close in age, Kevin should look like he could be married to Jamie. Carl's age is flexible—it is interesting to play with different age possibilities for this character.

SETTING

The entirety of the play takes place in Jamie and Kevin's living room.

TIME

The play unfolds in real time, without intermission.

STAGING

BROTHER was originally staged in the round making use of the entire theater as the playing space. The audience sat on folding chairs along the walls of the theater, which served as the walls of the apartment. The windows of the theater were the windows of the apartment, the door was actually the door to the outside, etc... Everyone was lit, actors and audience alike. The intimacy and grounding in reality worked well with the piece and added to the inherent tension of the work.

AUTHOR'S NOTE

BROTHER was originally performed in the round using the entirety of a loft-like theater as playing space. We kept candles on every surface, candy, nail polish, decks of cards.... The space felt lived in and actors had options. That said, this play was written to be somewhat flexible. The staging and blocking should reflect what best fits the space you have to work with.

The more stuff there is around for actors to handle the better.

There are certain lines in the script that contain details that add authenticity. We purchased a different kind of generic cake each night (*Buttered Sunshine* in the script) and Kevin would call out whatever he found in the bag as he entered. It kept things spontaneous and fun. At another point, Carl makes a reference to the weather, saying, "It's hot". That line should change to describe the weather at the time of your performance. He can say, "It's cold," or "It's raining." The date of Jamie's birthday (July 21 in the script) should be updated daily to be the actual performance date.

Carl's *Noodleman* voice should be the actor's own creation and I would encourage him to change it up. Have fun with it. Ditto the dance routine—Jamie and Margeaux can make up their own routine and practice it.

Use music you can rightly get your hands on during the play. In addition to the dance scene, we had music fade in as the lights went down at the end.

We began the play in several different ways—Jamie and Margeaux enter during blackout, Jamie and Margeaux start on stage as the audience enters, Jamie and Margeaux walk out while the audience is seated. My personal favorite was the latter—a couple minutes before the house closes, Jamie walks out and starts fixing her drink. Margeaux wanders in and plops down on the couch. The house closes.

(An East Village loft with a mix of grown-up furniture and Ikea pieces: miss-matched couch, chairs, and rugs, a coffee table, scattered newspapers, an empty wine bottle, a credenza with bottles of alcohol on top, lots of pictures around, a couple bookshelves full to capacity, a stereo, TV, an anatomical poster and several paintings on the wall, a couple of sad-looking plants and a cordless phone by the window.

The phone rings.

MARGEAUX lounges on the couch, flipping through a magazine. She wears a sexy top and short skirt, visible make-up, her high heels and large gold bag are on the floor.

JAMIE enters and walks to the credenza. She wears yoga pants, a tank top and cheap Chinese slippers.

JAMIE opens the credenza and takes two glasses out.

The phone continues to ring.

JAMIE fills one glass with ice, and pours vodka into it.

The phone continues to ring.

JAMIE glances at MARGEAUX. MARGEAUX stays with the magazine. JAMIE slices a lime, sucks on a piece.

The ringing grows annoying.

She drops her knife and goes to the phone. Just as she answers, the ringing stops.)

MARGEAUX. This feels like high school.

(Pause.)

JAMIE. I don't really drink.

(She hands the drink to MARGEAUX.)

MARGEAUX. Do you have any juice?
JAMIE. There's tomato juice.
MARGEAUX. Never mind.

(MARGEAUX lights a cigarette.)

JAMIE. You can't smoke in here.
MARGEAUX. There's an ashtray right there.
JAMIE. I know, but, I quit.

(She stamps out MARGEAUX's cigarette and throws it away. MARGEAUX stands with the drink and walks around the room.)

JAMIE. Hungry?
MARGEAUX. Not really. I've sort of been snacking all day.
JAMIE. Yeah, me too.

(Pause.)

JAMIE. I could make you an omelet.
MARGEAUX. Yeah. No thanks.

(She stops in front of the anatomical poster.)

MARGEAUX. I always wanted to be a surgeon. Suture things. Apply pressure. Rip somebody's heart out.
JAMIE. You have to go to school for a long time for that.
MARGEAUX. So?
JAMIE. I'm just saying.
MARGEAUX. What?
JAMIE. Given your record...

(Pause.)

MARGEAUX. This makes no sense. The frame is completely wrong for the picture.
JAMIE. What?
MARGEAUX. It's black for one thing. There's nothing in this room that would suggest black.

JAMIE.	MARGEAUX.
Why were you running?	These are things you need to
Before. Downstairs.	consider. Colors, wood grain...
	Spacial relationships.
It seemed like—	It was raining. Duh.

JAMIE. But you were already wet.
MARGEAUX. I didn't want to get wet-er.
JAMIE. Was there someone behind you?

(CARL enters just enough for JAMIE and MARGEAUX to see him.)

CARL. Have you got a plunger?

(MARGEAUX laughs.)

JAMIE. In the closet by the sink.

(He exits.)

MARGEAUX. That is my worst nightmare.
JAMIE. It's... whatever. It happens.
MARGEAUX. Not if I can help it. Every night, before bed, I drink a glass of Metamucil. I wake up, I'm on the toilet. *My* toilet.
JAMIE. That's...
MARGEAUX. I don't like public toilets.
JAMIE. Just public or other peoples'?
MARGEAUX. Both, but, I make exceptions. The library is all right.
JAMIE. My friend Natia won't go at her boyfriend's.
MARGEAUX. How long've they been together?
JAMIE. Six months.
MARGEAUX. That's a bit much.
JAMIE. It's ridiculous.
MARGEAUX. I don't think so. There are boundaries. Or there should be. *(pause)* I had this guy pick me up for a first date. He took a shit before we even got out the door. It was very strange.
JAMIE. How did you know?
MARGEAUX. I knew.
JAMIE. How?
MARGEAUX. I... heard things.
JAMIE. What kinds of things?
MARGEAUX. You're disgusting.

(JAMIE laughs.)

JAMIE. *(pouring herself a drink)* I was at Michael last Sunday—

MARGEAUX.	JAMIE.
I hate that place. A rat ran across my foot in that place.	The toilet wouldn't flush. And I'd had a LOT of coffee.

(Pause.)

JAMIE. I'd been messed up all week, too much soy... So there was like three days worth that had... and they were these long, firm—
MARGEAUX. All right.
JAMIE. I fished them out with my hands and threw them in the trash.

(Pause.)

JAMIE. I always wanted to be a surgeon, rip somebody's heart out, suture things... apply pressure.
MARGEAUX. *I* wanted to be a surgeon.
JAMIE. Yeah. No thanks.
MARGEAUX. You were running.
JAMIE. I don't like public toilets.
MARGEAUX. I was at Michael.
JAMIE. I hate that place.
MARGEAUX. The toilet wouldn't flush.
JAMIE. It was very strange.
MARGEAUX. Was someone following you?

(CARL enters wearing a shirt and pants that are clearly too

small.)

CARL. I left the...
JAMIE. Great. I'm gonna get us something to eat.
MARGEAUX. I'm really not hungry.
JAMIE. Maybe...
CARL. Carl.

JAMIE.	MARGEAUX.
...is hungry.	Carl?

(JAMIE brushes past CARL as she exits.)

CARL. What?
MARGEAUX. No, it's just... You look like... I guess I thought it would be something more ethnic.

(CARL goes to the big chair.)

CARL. Like what?
MARGEAUX. Jamal... Kwame... DuPont.
CARL. DuPont?
MARGEAUX. Yeah, you know, like one of those made-up sounding ones.
CARL. No, no, I don't think I do.
MARGEAUX. Shenequa, LaTanya, Beyonce...

(JAMIE enters with a bowl of pork rinds.)

CARL. Oh, you mean, like, um, wait wait wait... Cody? Caitlin. Ethan? Ava.

MARGEAUX. My uncle has a dog named Cody.
JAMIE. So, you're not hungry? How about TV? You wanna watch TV?

MARGEAUX.	CARL.
You got cable?	I should check on my suit.
JAMIE.	MARGEAUX.
No, but , I get the channels.	There's no way it's dry.

JAMIE. The cable guy split my internet, so the local ones come in pretty well.

(She turns on the TV.)

MARGEAUX. Why would he do that?
JAMIE. I don't know.
MARGEAUX. He liked you.
JAMIE. I don't think so.
MARGEAUX. Did you fuck him?
JAMIE. What?
MARGEAUX. It's a fair question.
JAMIE. I don't like you.
CARL. Scientific Maps.

(Quick pause.)

CARL. There was a college basketball player a few years back named Scientific Maps.
MARGEAUX. I don't even know how to begin to respond to that.
CARL. Had a brother called Majestic. Majestic Maps.

JAMIE. I'd say that tops DuPont.
CARL. Beats the pants off it.
JAMIE. He must've had a nickname.
CARL. I didn't read about a nickname.
JAMIE. They all have nicknames. SciMa? Smaps?
MARGEAUX. S & M.

(CARL laughs.)

CARL. S & M. I like that.
MARGEAUX. Most people claim to.
CARL. You're for real?
MARGEAUX. Bend over and lick my toenails 'cause I'm gonna make you scrub the floor with my toothbrush until it's clean enough to eat off. And then you'll stay locked in the cabinet until I say it's time to come out. Then maybe I'll wash your hair.
CARL. No shit.

(MARGEAUX shrugs.)

CARL. My, my, my. *(pause)* Reminds me of that Secretary movie, the part about the—

(JAMIE turns off the TV.)

JAMIE. She doesn't really do that. You don't really do that.
MARGEAUX. How do you know? *(pause)* Do you know?

(Pause.)

JAMIE. No.

(MARGEAUX smiles.)

JAMIE. You can go if...
MARGEAUX. Relax.

(JAMIE crosses to the credenza, refills her wine glass.)

MARGEAUX. Can I just ask one question?
JAMIE. No.
MARGEAUX. The cable guy...
JAMIE. Get out.
MARGEAUX. I was kidding. Jesus. Don't be so touchy.
JAMIE. I want you to leave.
MARGEAUX. Relax.
JAMIE. Now.
MARGEAUX. Where do you want me to go?
JAMIE. I don't care. Home.
MARGEAUX. I can't go home.
JAMIE. It's not even—
MARGEAUX. I got evicted.

(CARL snorts.)

JAMIE. What? When?
MARGEAUX. Three weeks ago.

(Pause.)

JAMIE. Where have you been sleeping?

MARGEAUX. You don't need to worry about that.
JAMIE. Margeaux—
MARGEAUX. With friends. At the gym.
JAMIE. The gym?
MARGEAUX. It's open 24hrs. And the massage rooms have tables. I can't really sleep anyway.
CARL. You spring for a gym with massage tables but you can't make rent?
MARGEAUX. Well, it's an annual membership isn't it.
JAMIE. Why didn't you call? *(crosses to the couch)* You could have called.
MARGEAUX. I guess I'm not quite clear on the rules.
JAMIE . There aren't rules...
MARGEAUX. No?
JAMIE. No.

(JAMIE sits next to MARGEAUX.)

CARL. You know each other.
MARGEAUX. You're quick.
JAMIE. You should have called. I left a message when we moved.
MARGEAUX. That was very kind of you.

(MARGEAUX takes her shoes and bag to chair by stereo.)

JAMIE. Do Mom and Dad know?
MARGEAUX. *(puts her shoes on)* Mom and Dad.
CARL. You two are... sisters? You look nothing alike.
MARGEAUX. I was adopted.
JAMIE. What? You were not. She was not.

MARGEAUX. Where are the pictures?
JAMIE. Margeaux.
MARGEAUX. We have pictures of you all bloody and umbilical.

(CARL moves to bookshelf.)

JAMIE. Grow up. *(pause)* He forgot his camera. *(pause)* I remember them bringing you home.
MARGEAUX. That doesn't prove anything.
JAMIE. You were wrapped in a yellow blankie.
MARGEAUX. I would like photographic evidence.
JAMIE. There are plenty of pictures of you crying.
CARL. You two are funny. The way you... It's crazy.

(He takes a book down, flips through.)

JAMIE. Careful who you call crazy.
MARGEAUX. Yeah, who are you?
JAMIE. Don't change the subject. I want to know what happened with Marcus. *(pause)* And where are the cats?
CARL. Who's Marcus?
JAMIE. Her boyfriend.
MARGEAUX. Ex-boyfriend. He's gone.
JAMIE. More.
MARGEAUX. He left.

CARL.	JAMIE.
(makes a noise)	Margeaux, I swear to God.

MARGEAUX. There was an incident.

JAMIE. Yes.
MARGEAUX. Which was not exactly my fault.
JAMIE. I'm sure it wasn't.
MARGEAUX. I got home late from this work party. I hadn't called cause I thought I'd be home early. I'd had a lot of these blue drinks. I walked into the apartment, dropped my bag in the living room, and passed out in bed. *(pause)* The next thing I know, I'm being shaken awake by a policeman and there's this scared-looking girl standing behind him crying.
JAMIE. What?
MARGEAUX. I was in 12E.
JAMIE. Oh my god...
MARGEAUX. Her front door was open! Who leaves their front door open in New York?
CARL. 12E.

(CARL suppresses a smile.)

JAMIE. It's not funny.
MARGEAUX. Well. I don't think it's funny at all. It was very traumatic.
JAMIE. I'm sure it was. For *her*.
MARGEAUX. I was shaken awake by a cop!
JAMIE. You crawled into her bed, drunk, in the middle of the night!
MARGEAUX. They nearly arrested me!
JAMIE. I would've arrested you!
CARL. What happened?
MARGEAUX. Well, we put two and two together—
CARL. You and the cops.

(JAMIE laughs.)

MARGEAUX. You are assholes.

(She grabs her bag, heads for the door.)

JAMIE. *(stopping her)* No, no, c'mon, tell us.

MARGEAUX. *(at the door)* They had my wallet. They saw on my license that I lived in the building. Of course they were curious as to why I was in 12E rather than 14...

JAMIE. All right. So, you're an idiot.

MARGEAUX. Well, here's the ironic part... *(She turns back.)* My door is locked, and, I don't have my keys. The cops won't leave until I'm inside. So we ring until Marcus opens the door, which isn't long, because it turns out he's been awake calling everybody I work with. I believe he told Gerald Sachs' wife to fuck herself.

CARL.	MARGEAUX.
Who's Gerald Sachs?	He gets all high and mighty, tells
JAMIE.	me I have a drinking problem.
The president of Singer	That I'm out of control.
Sachs.	

MARGEAUX. I started throwing all my stuff out the windows, down the trash chute. He just sat there. When my stuff was gone, I started on everything I'd ever given him. *(pause)* I flushed 'Finneas' down the toilet.

CARL.	JAMIE.
Who's Finneas?	Margeaux!

MARGEAUX. Marcus rescued him. The marbles from his bowl clogged the toilet. *(quick pause)* That was pretty much it. He took off on his motorcycle and when he got back, he said he was done. The apartment was paid till the end of the month. He sent movers the next day.

(Pause.)

JAMIE. What about the cats?
MARGEAUX. He took them. I said he could. They always liked him better anyway.
JAMIE. And your job?
MARGEAUX. There was a voice mail on my phone from Gerald's secretary.
JAMIE. I'm sorry.
MARGEAUX. I'm over it.
JAMIE. Don't say that.
MARGEAUX. Why not? It's in the past.
JAMIE. You're really good at that.
MARGEAUX. What?
JAMIE. I remembered something.

(JAMIE exits.)

MARGEAUX. Where're you going?
JAMIE. *(offstage)* I'll be right back.

(Pause.)

CARL. That's some psycho shit, flushing a fish down the toilet.

MARGEAUX. It was a crime of passion. I loved that fish.
CARL. Goldfish?
MARGEAUX. Japanese fighting fish.
CARL. Little colored thing? Those things are mean.
MARGEAUX. Only to other fighting fish. He let me pet him.
CARL. You pet a fish?
MARGEAUX. I would sort of stroke... Never mind.
CARL. No, no, no. This is interesting.

(MARGEAUX crosses to credenza.)

MARGEAUX. Do you have any pets?
CARL. No.
MARGEAUX. You live alone?
CARL. Sort of.
MARGEAUX. Do you, ever, *answer* a question?
CARL. I find talking is overrated.
MARGEAUX. You prefer to rap?

(Pause.)

CARL. Bitches and hos do'know one from the other. Momma left the crib gotta find me another.
MARGEAUX. You don't scare me.
CARL. I like that. *(He moves towards MARGEAUX.)* I like you.
MARGEAUX. You know downstairs? I didn't even see you. It was like you were part of the building.
CARL. We both know that's not true.

(JAMIE enters with a bottle of wine.)

JAMIE. I'm terrible with these things. Could you...

(CARL takes the bottle. MARGEAUX crosses to the big chair.)

CARL. Sure you want to open this?
JAMIE. Yeah. Why? Is it not good?
CARL. No, it should be real good. If you want...
JAMIE. Yeah, I mean... You'll have some, won't you?
MARGEAUX. You know me.
JAMIE. I have glasses.

(She opens the credenza.)

CARL. You've got a lot of glasses.
JAMIE. Oh. Yeah.

(CARL opens the bottle.)

JAMIE. You know a lot about wine?
CARL. Not a lot.
JAMIE. Well. I know nothing. Except that I like red.

(CARL pours a glass of wine. He swirls it, sniffs, sips noisily, swishes it in his mouth, and then swallows.)

MARGEAUX. Does that really do anything?
CARL. What?
MARGEAUX. The whole...

(She mimics his noisy swishy-sip.)

CARL. It, uh, I guess it makes you look like you know what you're doing. *(pause)* What do you think?
JAMIE. It's good. I like it. I don't really know though.
MARGEAUX. I think it could stand to breathe.

(He tastes it again.)

CARL. You're right.

(Pause.)

JAMIE. So, what do you think you'll do?
MARGEAUX. Hm?
JAMIE. You can't live like you're living.
MARGEAUX. It's not so bad.
JAMIE. Oh, come on. Crashing on couches, sleeping at the gym...
MARGEAUX. When you put it that way.
JAMIE. If you want—
MARGEAUX. Thanks. I'm sure I'll sort it out.
JAMIE. I'm terrible at that. Staying with people. I never know when I'm supposed to shower or what time to go to bed. *(She moves to couch.)* When I was little, I could never make it through sleepovers. Dad always had to pick me up at the last minute.
MARGEAUX. You always called right when he'd gotten to bed.
CARL. How old are you?
MARGEAUX. Twenty-nine. *(pause)* Happy Birthday.
CARL. It's your birthday?
JAMIE. It's not my birthday. Yet. I was born at six a.m.

MARGEAUX. La di da.
JAMIE. It makes a difference. *(pause)* What time were you born?
CARL. I have no idea.
JAMIE. Your parents never... My mom wakes up at six a.m. every July 21st, like clockwork.
CARL. You believe that?
JAMIE. What?
MARGEAUX. It's sweet.
CARL. It's pretty unlikely. 'Less she sets an alarm.
JAMIE. She does not set an alarm! *(pause)* It's a nice story.
MARGEAUX. It is.
CARL. How old are you?
MARGEAUX. Twenty-six.
CARL. That's funny. I thought you were older.

JAMIE.	MARGEAUX.
Thank you.	Thank you.

(Long pause.)

JAMIE. We should dance. I never dance. *(She goes to the stereo.)* Have a party... It would help if I knew how to work this. *(Music plays.)* Okay... *(She dances.)* Come on. I know *you* can dance. Shake that ass. *(pause)* Come on. *(pause)* Up! *(She pulls MARGEAUX up.)* Do that... Let's do that thing we used to do.

(JAMIE starts to do a dance.)

MARGEAUX. No...
JAMIE. Why not?

MARGEAUX. It's stupid.
JAMIE. You made it up.
MARGEAUX. I know but... There doesn't have to be a routine.

(Pause.)

JAMIE. I'm gonna change.

(JAMIE exits.)

MARGEAUX. This is... I didn't want to say anything before, but, $2800? For this place? *(pause)* It's not like it's big. My place was double this size. And that's dry wall. One good punch... *(She punches the wall.)* Ow!
CARL. Jesus...
JAMIE. *(Offstage.)* What was that?
MARGEAUX. Nothing.
CARL. Are you all right?
MARGEAUX. Yes. Don't touch me.

(Pause.)

CARL. You dented it.
MARGEAUX. Guess I don't know my own strength.
CARL. That's not dry wall.
MARGEAUX. Apparently not.
CARL. Lemme see it.
MARGEAUX. No.

(JAMIE enters wearing a sexy pink nightie.)

CARL. That's nice.
JAMIE. Thanks. I've had it forever. *(pause)* You okay?
MARGEAUX. Yeah. *(pause)* Actually... Could I lie down for a minute.
JAMIE. Of course.

(MARGEAUX exits. JAMIE turns the music up.)

JAMIE. Much better. I feel free...
CARL. You oughtta turn that down.
JAMIE. What?
CARL. It's too loud.
JAMIE. I can't hear you.

(JAMIE dances closer to CARL. Her back is to the front door when KEVIN enters. KEVIN wears a button-down shirt and nice pants. CARL sees him and steps away from JAMIE.)

KEVIN. *(screaming)* You can hear it starting on two!

(He turns off the music.)

JAMIE. Hi.
KEVIN. Hi.
JAMIE. Hi.
KEVIN. Yeah, hi.
JAMIE. Those for me?
KEVIN. Yeah. Happy Birthday.
JAMIE. Thank you. *(She takes the flowers.)* You're home early.

KEVIN. I got off early. *(JAMIE kisses KEVIN.)* I tried calling you. A few times. *(pause)* Hello.
CARL. Hey.
JAMIE. This is—
CARL. Carl. Carl Borden.
KEVIN. Kevin Murphy. *(pause)* Why is he wearing my clothes?
CARL. My—
JAMIE. They're not... They're from the pile you said I could give away.

(Quick pause.)

KEVIN. I should keep that shirt.
JAMIE. Carl's locked out. He's staying with Elena and Rick. He's Rick's brother from... out of town.
KEVIN. I didn't know Rick had a brother.
JAMIE. Oh, you've talked about that kind of thing?
KEVIN. What?
JAMIE. *(crossing to stereo)* Kevin's shy.
KEVIN. Where are they?
JAMIE. Out of town.
CARL. At a wedding.
KEVIN. Oh. Whose wedding?
JAMIE. A friend of Elena's.
CARL. College friend. Lucy. Her roommate.

(Pause.)

KEVIN. Lousy timing. You're here, they're gone.
CARL. Oh, yeah, well, they'll be back.

KEVIN. Did you call a locksmith?

(JAMIE turns on softer music.)

JAMIE. Not yet. We were just gonna do that.
KEVIN. You drank the Chateauneuf?
JAMIE. It was on top. *(She starts to dance.)* It's my birthday.
KEVIN. How was it?
JAMIE. Good.
KEVIN. Good? *(KEVIN grabs JAMIE from behind. They sway to the music.)* I'm glad it was *good*.

(He twirls her away from the stereo and turns it off, crosses to the couch and sits.)

KEVIN. I love this couch.

(Pause.)

JAMIE. How was work?
KEVIN. Eh. You know. Heiney yelling at his French wife. *(As KEVIN speaks, JAMIE goes to the credenza. CARL hands her a vase. Their hands touch. She crosses back to the TV and arranges the flowers beside it.)* She calls to tell him she got in a fender-bender.... It wasn't her fault and she's fine, but she's upset, you know. She was driving his car and it got scratched or something. She wants him to say it's okay, but he starts asking her all these questions—where she was when it happened, where she was on her way to... And then he's yelling at her, not about the car, he doesn't even care about the scratch, he's all puffed up about the route she took home from Jack's. "Why in god's name

would you take the interstate?! It's a clear shot on back roads. Only a moron would take 95 that time of day! CELINE... CELINE? ARE YOU LISTENING TO ME? ARE YOU LISTENING, CELINE?" *(mocking "Rocky")* CELEEEEEENE! *(he laughs)* That fuckin' guy. Best part of the job.

JAMIE. He sounds like an asshole.

KEVIN. He is, but it's not... He's not mean-spirited about it.

JAMIE. I don't know why you stay there.

KEVIN. Nobody bothers me. It's a good deal.

CARL. What do you do?

KEVIN. Paralegal.

CARL. Oh. *(pause)* What, uh, what is that? You hear about it on TV.

(JAMIE laughs.)

KEVIN. It can mean different things—I draft and manage documents to support very complex litigation.

JAMIE. Basically a legal secretary.

KEVIN. Not a legal secretary.

CARL. You like it?

KEVIN. I like it fine.

JAMIE. *(moving to KEVIN)* He went to law school. He's passed the bar. He insists on working nights as a legal temp.

(JAMIE crosses to KEVIN.)

KEVIN. I like to keep my days free.

JAMIE. What for?

KEVIN. If I worked days I wouldn't get to hang out with you.

JAMIE. You'd get to sleep. *(She straddles him.)* He never

sleeps.
KEVIN. Sleep.

(JAMIE kisses KEVIN.)

CARL. I work nights.
KEVIN. See?
JAMIE. Do you do it by choice? Kevin chooses to keep vampire hours.
KEVIN. *(lifts her off his lap, moves to credenza)* I make double overtime and I get to associate with guys like Heiney. Guys like that don't work the day shift.
JAMIE. No shit.
KEVIN. *(fixes a whisky on the rocks)* I switched to days. Wanted to kill myself. Day people take themselves way too seriously. It's all about getting this and that done by 5 o'clock. Rush rush rush. Like little mice. At night, you set your own pace. You get donuts from the bakery when they make 'em fresh at 2 AM. I'm my own boss baby.
JAMIE. So you say.
KEVIN. Do I not provide for you? Do I not buy you the finest silks and the choicest morsels?
JAMIE. It's not about the money.
KEVIN. Everything's about money. Jamie has expensive tastes, whether or not she likes to admit it.
JAMIE. That's not true.
KEVIN. Belize, Santorini, diving the Great Barrier Reef...
JAMIE. I like adventures, but I don't buy things. I don't acquire possessions.
KEVIN. She throws everything away. Keep an eye on your...
JAMIE. I throw things away because you bring home junk.

Last week, he dragged an armoire up here in the middle of the night with the guy from the deli.

KEVIN. It was a nice piece.

JAMIE. It had no drawers.

KEVIN. Adventures are expensive. Not that I'm complaining. You look hot in a wet suit.

JAMIE. Oh, and if I didn't?

KEVIN. Diving would be out of the question.

JAMIE. Fucker.

KEVIN. You asked, baby.

(She goes to him.)

JAMIE. You wouldn't love me if I weighed 300 pounds?

KEVIN. I'd love you, I just wouldn't wanna see you in a wet suit. It's like fat people in spandex—Why?

JAMIE. You're terrible.

KEVIN. You love it. *(They kiss.)* Grab another bottle.

JAMIE. Which one?

KEVIN. Doesn't matter. *(JAMIE starts for the kitchen.)* Not the Petrus. *(She exits.)*

(KEVIN crosses to the big chair.)

KEVIN. So, Carl, where are you in town from?

(CARL moves to credenza.)

CARL. New Jersey.

KEVIN. New Jersey? That's hardly—

CARL. Southern New Jersey. Far to the South.

KEVIN. Down by Cape May?
CARL. Yeah. Close to there.
KEVIN. I love that area.
CARL. It's a nice area.
KEVIN. We used to vacation in Ocean City. They got a ferry to Cape May. You ever take that ferry?
CARL. I'm not much for boats.
KEVIN. Lotta people get seasick.
CARL. I can't swim.
KEVIN. They've got life jackets you know. They're required by law to have them on board.
CARL. I think it's the distance from the shore.
KEVIN. So, if the boat were docked...
CARL. That might be okay.

(MARGEAUX enters.)

KEVIN. That's a good sign. You might get your sea legs yet. *(He notices MARGEAUX.)* GET THE FUCK OUT!
MARGEAUX. *(sitting)* Hello Kevin.

(JAMIE enters with a bottle of wine.)

JAMIE. Is that my shirt?
MARGEAUX. Oh, yeah, mine was wet. I tried to find one that looked like you didn't wear it much.
JAMIE. Yeah, it's new. I haven't worn it yet.

MARGEAUX.	KEVIN.
Oh. Well, I'll dry-clean it for you.	HEY!

MARGEAUX. Kevin you're turning red.
KEVIN. *(standing)* Don't say my name! DO NOT SPEAK MY NAME.
MARGEAUX. Or what?
KEVIN. I'm not kidding.
MARGEAUX. You're so dramatic. *(pause)* Kevin. *(KEVIN grabs MARGEAUX by the hair, pulling her out of her chair.)* Ow!
JAMIE. Kevin!

(CARL grabs KEVIN, pinning his arms behind his back.)

MARGEAUX.	KEVIN.
Wow. Did you see that?	Get off me! GET OFF!

KEVIN. This is my house!

MARGEAUX.	KEVIN.
She lives here too! He's always doing that.	Did you let her in?

JAMIE. Yes.
KEVIN. Unbelievable.

MARGEAUX.	JAMIE.
Eat me!	Margeaux.
KEVIN.	
Don't make me puke.	Stop it.

KEVIN. I want her out!

(MARGEAUX moves to the back door.)

JAMIE. You're acting like a baby.
KEVIN. Me?
JAMIE. Yes!
KEVIN. She's not supposed to be here!
JAMIE. Well, she's here.
MARGEAUX. In your house.
JAMIE. Margeaux.
MARGEAUX. Sorry.

(Pause.)

JAMIE. Let him go.
CARL. You sure?

(JAMIE nods. CARL releases KEVIN. KEVIN wheels around to face CARL.
Pause.
KEVIN exits.)

MARGEAUX. He brought you flowers.
JAMIE. He always does.
MARGEAUX. That's sweet.
CARL. Last time I brought a woman flowers she bit one off and swallowed it.
MARGEAUX. I've never had a guy bring me flowers.
CARL. Never?
MARGEAUX. Not without asking for them first.
JAMIE. Kevin's good like that. Be nice please.
MARGEAUX. I was. *(pause)* I will.

(JAMIE refills her wine.)

MARGEAUX. *(Calling to KEVIN)* Too bad you had to work all night on your wife's birthday. *(JAMIE looks at MARGEAUX.)* They should give you a night off.

(KEVIN enters.)

KEVIN. Do you hear something? It seems like someone's talking, but, it's 4 AM and I can't imagine why there would be anyone in my house.

(He pours himself some wine.)

KEVIN. Now that you're not practicing your kung-fu death grip, who are you tough guy?
CARL. I'm not anybody.
KEVIN. I'm sure that's probably true. Especially considering my sister-in-law here. Nobody who's anybody would bother with her.
MARGEAUX. Fuck you.
JAMIE. Margeaux.
MARGEAUX. He needs to let it go.
KEVIN. Oh, I need to let it go? I need to let it go?
MARGEAUX. Yes.
KEVIN. You're in my house!

(Pause.)

MARGEAUX. Sorry?

(Pause.)

KEVIN. I'm not a violent man.

JAMIE. She said sorry.
KEVIN. Never got in a single fight growing up. Bet you got in some fights.

(JAMIE crosses to small bookshelf.)

CARL. A couple.
KEVIN. Yeah. *(pause)* I wouldn't a been much good at fighting. Slow reflexes. That thing you did before? I couldn't do that.
JAMIE. Would you stop doing that?
KEVIN. What?
JAMIE. Selling yourself short. You're always apologizing for things before it's necessary.
KEVIN. What?
JAMIE. Like at dinner the other night, when that guy asked you to play racquetball, what did you say?
KEVIN. I said I couldn't afford it.
JAMIE. Exactly.
KEVIN. It's true. We can't afford the dues at that club.
JAMIE. He wasn't asking you to join the fucking club! He wanted you to play one game! You could've just said yes. You have to go and say you can't afford it and make everybody uncomfortable.
KEVIN. I wasn't the least bit uncomfortable.
JAMIE. I was. And he was. And his wife was.
KEVIN. I don't want to commit to something I can't do.
JAMIE. It's not a commitment! It's just a thing, that people say. It's conversation. No one means anything they say.
KEVIN. Are you listening to yourself?
JAMIE. You know what I mean.
KEVIN. You want me to lie.

KEVIN. You want me to lie.
JAMIE. Not lie, just... Be less...
KEVIN. What? *(pause)* Don't distract her she's onto something.

(Pause.)

JAMIE. I don't know.
KEVIN. That's it? That's the grand finale?
JAMIE. I don't want to embarrass you. I know how easily you're embarrassed.
KEVIN. Oh. I see. *(pause)* Well.

(KEVIN exits.)

JAMIE. It always ends that way.

(Pause.)

MARGEAUX. I'm sorry if...
JAMIE. It's not you. I mean... You know. *(pause)* Bet you're sorry you walked into this house.
CARL. Why?
JAMIE. Problems.
CARL. Those aren't problems.

(Pause.)

JAMIE. Do you want some of this?

(MARGEAUX comes down from the doorway.)

MARGEAUX. Sure.
JAMIE. So... What were we talking about?
MARGEAUX. Birthdays?
CARL. We weren't talking we were dancing.

(Pause.)

JAMIE. I'll be right back.

(JAMIE exits.)

CARL. What's the... elephant?
MARGEAUX. Sorry?
CARL. Why are you the black sheep?
MARGEAUX. Oh. It's stupid.
CARL. Not to Legal Aide.
MARGEAUX. No, not to him.

(Pause.)

CARL. Am I supposed to guess?
MARGEAUX. I don't play games.
CARL. No?
MARGEAUX. Not usually.
CARL. I'm flattered.
MARGEAUX. Why?
CARL. To be the exception.
MARGEAUX. This has nothing to do with you. *(She freshens her drink.)* I had keys to their old place, for emergencies or whatever. I would go over there sometimes, between classes, to shower and nap, watch soaps... Jamie knew. I was there one time

napping and Kevin came home and... *(pause)* He's just too controlling. I bought her a vibrator for Christmas and he threw it away. He wouldn't have been so quick to if he'd seen the instructional video that came with it.

(Pause.)

    CARL. You ever do that?
    MARGEAUX. What?
    CARL. You know.
    MARGEAUX. Masturbate or watch porn?
    CARL. The first one.
    MARGEAUX. Who doesn't. *(pause)* Oh come on.
    CARL. It's a sin.
    MARGEAUX. You're telling me you don't jerk off.
    CARL. I'm not telling you anything.

(Pause.)

    MARGEAUX. You're serious.
    CARL. I didn't say anything.
    MARGEAUX. Wow.
    CARL. Not wow.
    MARGEAUX. How does that work?
    CARL. Never started.
    MARGEAUX. Huh. *(pause)* You're not a virgin, are you?
    CARL. No.
    MARGEAUX. No?
    CARL. No.
    MARGEAUX. Oh my god. This is unbelievable.
    CARL. It's not anything.

MARGEAUX. How old are you?
CARL. You're putting words in my mouth.
MARGEAUX. You're like a science experiment. A caveman? What am I trying to say?

CARL.	MARGEAUX.
Your ass…	I keep picturing dioramas.
I see your ass.	Installations.
I wanna get up in that and…	I feel dirty.
I'm gonna slap the shit outta you.	No, really, I… I've had a lot of sex.
Bitch.	I'm not kidding. Disgusting sex. Like—

(KEVIN enters.)

KEVIN. I'm going to get cake.

(He grabs his keys.)

CARL. Are there stores open this late?
KEVIN. Key Food. 24hrs.

(He exits.)

MARGEAUX. Do you mind if I shower? *(pause)* I've been walking around all night. And I'm cold. I'd like to shower.
JAMIE. Go ahead.

*(MARGEAUX exits.
JAMIE takes one of her cigarettes.)*

JAMIE. Want one?
CARL. No.

(She lights up, goes to the back door.)

JAMIE. I hate staying up late. *(She opens the door, smokes.)* But, I can't sleep, so... I turn on the shower. I eat cereal and I make coffee... If I want more cereal, I pretend the shower's not hot yet. Sometimes I let the water run and never get in. *(smokes)* I read the paper, but it makes me anxious. I feel like I should be doing something else. *(pause)* Let's go on the roof.
CARL. It's hot.
JAMIE. So? *(pause)* Never mind.

(She smokes.)

CARL. I'm sorry
JAMIE. I left the house this morning to—
CARL. *(moving to her)* I'm saying I'm sorry.

(Pause.)

JAMIE. Where did you come from?
CARL. Alaska.
JAMIE. Wow.
CARL. Yeah.
JAMIE. Are you an Eskimo?
CARL. No.
JAMIE. Of course not.

(JAMIE flicks her cigarette out, crosses to small bookshelf.)

CARL. I'm a doorman.
JAMIE. I know. I've... seen you.

(CARL shuts the door.)

CARL. You've seen me.
JAMIE. I've walked by. *(pause)* You like that? Working there?
CARL. It's all right.
JAMIE. I always wonder about that building. It seems out of place.
CARL. I just work there. *(pause)* You've walked by?
JAMIE. Of course. It's right around the corner.

(CARL crosses to small bookshelf.)

CARL. If I could take it back...

(JAMIE moves to credenza, her back to CARL.)

JAMIE. How much are units in there?
CARL. I would take it back.
JAMIE. $4000? At least, right? *(pause)* My parents have doormen. That they're friends with. One of them was a general in the Ethiopian army... Schiff.
CARL. Schiff?
JAMIE. Yeah. His brother works there too. Kafiri? I think. The one at night is a high school teacher. Kline. He teaches calculus. I think he sleeps some, since it's night. Do you sleep?
CARL. No.

(CARL approaches JAMIE.)

JAMIE. When I was in high school, there was one named William. *(pause)* William had the smallest head. This little Beetlejuice head. It was weird because he started having seizures, blacking out at work. And then they found a brain tumor.

(He stops right behind her.)

CARL. What happened to him?
JAMIE. He had surgery to remove it. He came back, and then... I don't know. He didn't come back.
CARL. What about the brother?
JAMIE. I don't know.
CARL. You never asked?

(She turns to face him.)

JAMIE. I went to college.

(Pause.)

CARL. I don't—
JAMIE. Me either. I never even talked to him. I mean, I said, "Hi," but... All of a sudden he's saying he always thought we'd end up together!
CARL. William?
JAMIE. That he thought we'd get married!
CARL. Why would he think that?
JAMIE. I have no idea!
CARL. Why are you telling me this?
JAMIE. He was a doorman. *(pause)* That's not... I didn't mean—

CARL. He was black.
JAMIE. That's not what—
CARL. A "brotha"?
JAMIE. No—
CARL. I'm not trying to marry you.
JAMIE. You approached me.
CARL. Not for this.
JAMIE. No? You weren't hoping to get inside.
CARL. No.
JAMIE. What for then? *(pause)* Why don't you say, *WHAT FOR?*

(Pause.)

CARL. I was lonely.

(KEVIN enters with a Key Food bag.)

KEVIN. "Buttered Sunshine" is all they had, so... *(pause)* Where is she?
JAMIE. Showering.
KEVIN. She's showering? What for?
JAMIE. Give it a rest.
KEVIN. Excuse me?
JAMIE. We get it.

(She crosses to stereo.)

KEVIN. I feel like I'm in the Twilight Zone.
CARL. I've been feeling that way all night.
KEVIN. An escape pod. I need an escape pod. *(He gets*

birthday candles) Were you smoking? *(pause)* Unbelievable. Your mother is dying of cancer, and you smoke.

JAMIE. Why do you ask if you know?

KEVIN. Why do you lie about it? *(He sits, opens the cake.)* It's just not healthy. You oughtta quit now, before... *(pause)* You too.

CARL. I don't smoke.

KEVIN. Good for you.

CARL. My momma said she'd kill me she ever saw me smoking. She said that with a True Blue hanging out of her mouth.

KEVIN. She smoked in the house?

CARL. When she was there.

KEVIN. That's awful.

CARL. Her house.

KEVIN. It's no environment for a kid.

CARL. I liked the smoke. It stayed in a room even after she left. *(pause)* She was down on her hands and knees one time, cleaning out my closet. I was standing behind her, watching her. She had on a summer dress, belted at the waist and her hair was up in combs.

JAMIE. What was your mother's name?

CARL. Cecilia.

JAMIE. Pretty.

KEVIN. That's—

CARL. She was strict. Too strict. You know what she hated the most? I used to do this thing during recess... *(He pulls his shirt up around his head, tucking his arms in so that his elbows are slung.)* ...I don't remember how it started, but, *("Noodleman voice")* Hello ladies. Do you have a kiss for Noodleman? Look at chyou. I could just eat chyou up. Like a pasta. With a meata balls. *(normal)* All the girls loved Noodleman. Except her. I think it was the voice that bothered her.

KEVIN. That's tough. Tough growing up in a house like that. *(pause)* I was pretty lucky I guess. Mom stayed home, Dad was there in time for dinner most nights. We didn't watch too much TV or eat sugar cereals.

JAMIE. Your parents hate each other.

KEVIN. That's not... First of all, that's not true, but, the point is, it wouldn't have mattered. They kept their problems separate.

JAMIE. Your dad drank a fifth of scotch every night.

KEVIN. Helped him relax.

JAMIE. Your mother disappeared for hours on end.

KEVIN. She was visiting with the neighbors. The neighborhood ladies.

JAMIE. Kevin...

KEVIN. Every night, I went to bed and I prayed that everything would stay just the way it was.

CARL. That's beautiful.

JAMIE. You don't have to do this. You were doing so well.

KEVIN. Jamie and her mother—

JAMIE. No.

KEVIN. Her father—

JAMIE. No more.

KEVIN. Why can't we hear about your parents?

JAMIE. We're done.

KEVIN. With what?

JAMIE. *(crosses to KEVIN)* I know what you're trying to say, but I'll pretend I don't so we can keep on talking. I'll tell you if you tell me. *(She sits.)* Tell me something real.

KEVIN. Have you been drinking? She's not supposed to drink.

JAMIE. What do you like about me?
KEVIN. What?
JAMIE. What do you like?
KEVIN. That's not...
JAMIE. I'm not mad. I'm just asking. What is it about me that you can't live without?
KEVIN. Honey...
JAMIE. You never call me that.

(He stands, moves behind her.)

KEVIN. You're my baby.
JAMIE. I don't know what that means.

(He rubs her shoulders.)

KEVIN. Tell her.
CARL. What?
KEVIN. You've got babies... Shorties...
JAMIE. Oh my god.
KEVIN. Tell her what it means.
JAMIE. Oh, my, god.

(MARGEAUX enters with wet hair.)

KEVIN.	MARGEAUX.
Ah-ha! Baby!	*(sings to the tune of "Happy Birthday," piecing it together:)* Feliz anniversaire, ton cumpleanos es... ilegaire... Tues Bonita y joven... y jet'amai bien.

MARGEAUX. I love you.
JAMIE. I love you too.

(KEVIN pushes MARGEAUX onto JAMIE's lap.)

KEVIN. What are you, a lesbian?
JAMIE. What?
KEVIN. Seem more interested in girls.
JAMIE. You're...
MARGEAUX. Mm... Let's eat it, I'm starving.

(She spoons icing off with her pinky.)

KEVIN. Where're you going?
CARL. I'm gonna take off.

JAMIE.	KEVIN.
What? Oh. Really.	Party pooper! You gotta stay for cake. And Margeaux. You've definitely gotta stay for Margeaux.
CARL.	MARGEAUX.
I would say it was nice meeting you...	He doesn't have to stay for me.
JAMIE.	KEVIN.
It was... I don't know what it was. I don't know... anything.	He's your guy, you go with him.

MARGEAUX. He's not mine.
KEVIN. Whatever you want to call it.
MARGEAUX. We're not together.

KEVIN. What?

MARGEAUX. I never saw him before tonight.

KEVIN. You're not...

MARGEAUX. He hit me before you got here.

JAMIE. That is not true.

MARGEAUX. You didn't hear what he said to me when you were in the bedroom.

KEVIN. What were you doing in the bedroom? *(pause)* Hello?

MARGEAUX. Jamie went to change clothes. DuPont, I mean, Carl and I stayed out here—

KEVIN. Who's DuPont? Was there someone else here?

JAMIE. No. *(pause)* You hit her?

CARL. Naw, she's confused.

MARGEAUX. Maybe it was a dream.

KEVIN. I'm confused.

JAMIE. Margeaux had a dream—

KEVIN. No. I'm confused about what you're doing in my house.

CARL. I came to use the bathroom.

KEVIN. The bathroom? Oh. Okay. *(pause)* What are you, off the street? Is this some street thing? Some gang bang?

JAMIE. Kevin.

KEVIN. Find a girl, follow her upstairs...

JAMIE. I invited him up.

Kevin. You invited—

JAMIE. Yes. I ran into him at Two Boots and the bathroom was broken. And then Margeaux was waiting at the apartment...

MARGEAUX. We were invited up.

KEVIN. You invited a stranger up to use the bathroom.

JAMIE. He wasn't... He works around the corner. We've met

before.

MARGEAUX. When Jamie's lying, she licks her lips. It's cute.

JAMIE. You don't know what you're talking about. *(crosses to credenza)* He works at the building around the corner. He came to use the bathroom. It was raining really hard so we had the wine to wait it out. Margeaux and I started fighting, and then you got home. That's it. Nothing happened.

KEVIN. That's all.

JAMIE. Yes.

KEVIN. Carl? Is that it?

JAMIE. Yes.

KEVIN. I'm asking him.

CARL. Yeah. That's it.

KEVIN. I don't know. I just don't know, Carl. Why'd she invite you up here? Why's she in a nightie? Why didn't she answer her phone all night long?

CARL. *(quietly)* Ask her.

KEVIN. What? You're gonna have to speak up monkey-boy. Those big lips are getting in your way.

(CARL looks KEVIN in the eye.)

CARL. I said, maybe you should ask her.

(Pause.)

KEVIN. You wanna fuck my wife?

JAMIE. Kevin!

KEVIN. Is that what's going on? You wanna spread her legs and thrust your cock into her wet pussy? I can't guarantee it'll be wet—

JAMIE. *(grabs his arm)* Stop it!

(KEVIN slaps JAMIE across the face. She stumbles backwards.)

KEVIN. This is why she doesn't drink. *(pause)* She's not supposed to drink. One drink is two, two drinks are four... *(pause)* She takes pills. For anxiety.
MARGEAUX. No wonder.

(Pause.)

KEVIN. Baby? Sorry baby. *(quick pause)* I'm an asshole. I don't know what came over me. Look at you. You're beautiful. You're so beautiful. And it's your birthday. *(pause)* Did I hurt you? Say I didn't hurt you?

(Pause.)

JAMIE. You didn't hurt me.
KEVIN. It's all better now?

(Pause.)

JAMIE. It's all better now.

(KEVIN claps his hands.)

KEVIN. Cake. *(He cuts the cake.)* Look at that. Looks good. *(pause)* Mmm mmm mmm. *(pause)* Sorry about... You understand though, it's late and... I worry, working nights. You understand.

CARL. Absolute.

(KEVIN takes a bite of cake.)

KEVIN. Can't be too careful.
CARL. Days aren't much better.
KEVIN. What's that?
CARL. I said, days aren't much better. Are they? All kindsa things can happen during the daylight hours. Unexpected kindsa things.

(KEVIN turns his back to CARL, continues cutting the cake.)

KEVIN. This isn't bad. For grocery store cake. Reminds me of boy scout barbecues. Or... cub scouts. I never made it to the boy scouts. *(MARGEAUX makes her way towards JAMIE.)* You know they wouldn't give me the badge for camping? I couldn't set up this goddamn tent they gave us. The poles were bent. I told them that, but they insisted... You can't make bent poles meet. It's not possible, but that information fell on deaf ears. Yep. No camping badge... I got all the others—archery, citizenship, cooking, sportsmanly conduct... *(pause)* Know what I can't figure? Why wouldn't they just give me the badge? Who was so intent on keeping a twelve-year-old from making boy scout? Who fuckin' cares if I couldn't put the tent up? It's not like tent set up is ever gonna save you. Now tying that bandana, that was...

(KEVIN hits CARL on the back of the head with the empty wine bottle. CARL drops to the floor.)

JAMIE. Oh my god!

KEVIN. I didn't do it.

(JAMIE runs to CARL.)

JAMIE. Carl? Oh, god... *(She puts her hand on his back.)* He's not breathing. Jesus Christ, Kevin!
KEVIN. There's no bathroom at Two Boots.
JAMIE. I don't... I can't remember this.
MARGEAUX. You have to break his ribs.

(JAMIE tries to turn him over.)

KEVIN. There's no bathroom!
MARGEAUX. Lean the head back.
JAMIE. I know, I just—
KEVIN. I came home early!
JAMIE. Call 911.
MARGEAUX. I can't. They'll ask my name.
JAMIE. Kevin. *(KEVIN picks up the phone.)* Kevin? *(pause)* Give it to me! *(pause)* I swear to god Kevin...
KEVIN. What are you going to say.
JAMIE. He's gonna die!
KEVIN. All the more reason.
JAMIE. Give me the phone! *(pause)* KEVIN?! *(KEVIN steps back holding the phone tight.)*

(JAMIE looks at CARL.)

JAMIE. *(piecing story together)* The buzzer rang. I thought it was the food I'd ordered. From the deli. A man came to the door and I opened it. He forced his way in... You got home just in time. You struggled and you hit him with the wine bottle. To protect me. You were trying to make things better.

(Pause.
KEVIN hands her the phone. She dials 911.)

    JAMIE. Margeaux.

(MARGEAUX grabs her bag and exits.)

    JAMIE. Hi... 2nd Street between A and B. Avenue A and Avenue B. A man isn't breathing. Jamie Chambers. 917-565-4289. No, I don't know how to do that. Yes. I'm willing.

(Music fades in as the lights fade to black.)

THE END

PROPERTY LIST

FURNITURE
couch
coffee table
chairs (5)
large bookshelf
small bookshelf
back bookshelf/table
credenza
TV stand/table
stereo stand/table
*table and chairs
*plant stand

PROPS
TV (practical)
stereo (practical)
trashcan
plants
framed photos (of cast members)
paintings
anatomy poster
keys (Kevin)
bag (Kevin)
bag (Carl, preset by TV)
purse (Margeaux, preset by couch)
lip gloss, clothes, brush, Vitamin C powder, etc... (Margeaux purse)
high heels (Margeaux, preset by couch)
pork rinds (backstage)

2 bottles red wine (backstage)
flowers (Kevin)
corkscrew (Jamie w/wine bottle 1)
birthday cake (Kevin, preset in grocery bag)

Credenza:
ice bucket/ice
rocks glasses
wine glasses
bottle of vodka
bottle of whisky
cutting board
knife
limes
birthday candles
cake knife
vase

Coffee table:
cigarettes & lighter
matches
breakaway wine bottle with Chateauneuf label
ashtray
newspaper
magazines

Small bookshelf:
playing cards
candles
wallet
books

chocolates in dish*
matches

Stereo stand:
stereo (or iPod speaker)
books and photos
candles
matches

Windowsill/back bookshelf:
plants
photos
trinkets
photo of Jamie and Kevin

*Front table:
keys
candles
gum

*these items are not essential but can add to the room.

COSTUME PLOT

Costume specifics should reflect the season. BROTHER was originally produced in the summer and the costume choices below reflect that. What's important is the overall feel of what each character is wearing.

JAMIE
Yoga pants
Tank top
Chinese slippers
Pink nightie

MARGEAUX
Sparkly top
Short skirt
High heels
Jeans
Button-down shirt

CARL
Tight t-shirt
Tight sweatpants
Sweat socks

KEVIN
Button-down shirt
Dress pants
Casual shoes

SET DRAWING

- exit
- front door
- audience
- audience
- stereo
- chair
- chair
- table
- chair
- audience
- TV
- small book shelf
- audience
- chair
- credenza
- book shelf
- coffee table
- couch
- chair
- audience
- anatomy poster
- steps
- audience
- window
- audience
- window
- back book shelf / plants
- back door

JUMP / CUT
Neena Beber

Winner of the L. Arnold Weissberger Award

Three bright urbanites want to make their mark on the world. Paul is a hardworking film-maker on the rise. His girlfriend Karen, a grad student, must get on with her thesis or find a life outside of academia. Dave, a life-long buddy whose brilliance is being consumed by increasingly severe episodes of manic-depression, is camping on Paul's couch. Paul and Karen decide to turn Paul into a documentary. The camera is on 24 hours a day, capturing up-close images of his jags and torpors and their responses. How far will love, friendship and ambition take this hip trio? "A remarkable, absorbing, complex and intelligent play."—*Variety*. 2 m., 1 f. (#12918)

STRANGER
Craig Lucas

Strangers on a transcontinental flight gradually reveal things they have never spoken about before: Linda is traveling with a great deal of cash as well as enough pills to kill herself; Hush has just been released from prison after serving fifteen years for kidnapping a young girl and keeping her alive inside a trunk for over a year. An alliance grows based on the shocking aspects of their personal histories. Together they go to a crude cabin in the middle of nowhere where they learn things about themselves and each other that change their lives irrevocably. A mystery, a tragedy, a love story, a requiem and a jaw-dropping shocker, *Stranger* is not suitable for bedtime reading. 2 m., 2 f. (#21446)

For more captivating dramas with small casts, see
THE BASIC CATALOGUE OF PLAYS AND MUSICALS
online at www.samuelfrench.com

DATE DUE

BRODART, CO.   Cat. No. 23-221-003

Samuel French Theater Bookshops

Specializing in plays and books on theater

45 West 25th Street
Second Floor
New York, NY 10010-2751
212 206 8990/FAX 212 206 1429

7623 Sunset Boulevard
Hollywood, CA 90046-2795
323 876 0570/FAX 323 876 6822

11963 Ventura Boulevard
Studio City, CA 91604-2607
818 762 0535

100 Lombard Street (Lower Level)
Toronto, Ontario M5C 1M3
CANADA
416 363 3536
FAX 416 363 1108

52 Fitzroy Street
London W1T 5JR
ENGLAND
011 44 20 7387 9373
FAX 011 44 20 7387 2161

e-mail: samuelfrench@earthlink.net   website: samuelfrench.com

ISBN   0 573 63224 3   #4758